T0100859

CYBER SPIES AND SECRET AGENTS OF MODERN TIMES

BY ALLISON LASSIEUR

Content Consultant:
Joseph Fitsanakis, PhD
Intelligence and National Security Studies Program
Coastal Carolina University

COMPASS POINT BOOKS
a capstone imprint

Compass Point Books are published by Capstone,
1710 Roe Crest Drive, North Mankato, Minnesota 56003
www.mycapstone.com

Copyright © 2017 by Compass Point Books, a Capstone imprint.
All rights reserved. No part of this publication may be reproduced in whole or in part, or stored in a
retrieval system, or transmitted in any form or by any means, electronic, mechanical, photocopying,
recording, or otherwise, without written permission of the publisher.

Library of Congress Cataloging-in-Publication Data
Names: Lassieur, Allison, author.
Title: Cyber spies and secret agents of modern times / by Allison Lassieur.
Description: North Mankato, Minnesota : Compass Point Books, [2017] | Series:
CPB grades 4–8. Spies! | Includes bibliographical references and index. | Audience: Ages 9–12.
Identifiers: LCCN 2016040418| ISBN 9780756554989 (library binding) |
ISBN 9780756555023 (pbk.) | ISBN 9780756555061 (ebook : .pdf)
Subjects: LCSH: Spies Juvenile literature. | Spies—History—21st century—Juvenile literature.
| Espionage—Juvenile literature. | Espionage—History—21st century—Juvenile literature. |
Espionage—Vocational guidance—Juvenile literature.
Classification: LCC UB270.5 .L38 2017 | DDC 327.12—dc23

LC record available at https://lccn.loc.gov/2016040418

Editorial Credits
Megan Atwood, editor; Russell Griesmer, designer; Tracey Engel, media researcher;
Steve Walker, production specialist

Photo Credits
Getty Images: 24, ALEXANDER NEMENOV, 16, Chip Somodevilla, 44, Daniel Berehulak, 36,
EMMANUEL DUNAND/AFP, 19, Greg Mathieson/Mai/Mai/The LIFE Images Collection, 46, Michael
Probst, 58, Photo by Cedric H. Rudisill/USAF/DOD, 12, Universal Images Group, 9; Newscom: Gene
Blevins/Polaris, 50, GUARDIAN/GLENN GREENWALD/LAURA POITRAS, 32, Laura Cavanaugh UPI
Photo Service, 6; Shutterstock: acid2728k, cover and 1 (code), Ensuper, design element, Fedorov Oleksiy,
design element, Freedom_Studio, design element, Here, design element, Kaissa, cover and 1 (cursor
icon), KPG_Euro, cover (silhouette), Monkey Business Images, 38, phokin, design element, pixelparticle,
cover and 1 (design element), pogonici, cover (laptop), Reddavebatcave, design element, scyther5, 26,
SkillUp, design element, STILLFX, design element, Vladitto, design element, xtock, cover (map)

Printed and bound in the USA
072019   000093

TABLE OF CONTENTS

In the age of social media and globalization, being a spy comes with a new set of challenges. In World War I, World War II, and the Cold War, spies had a specific nation or group of nations they worked against to win a war. As the world moved more into the digital age, the scope of spying became much broader. Today, enemies can be countries, terrorist groups, leagues of nations, or even individuals acting alone.

On September 11, 2001, the United States suffered one of the worst terrorist attacks the country had ever seen. The terrorist group, al-Qaida, consisted of a relatively small band of religious extremists bent on the destruction of the United States. Their successful terrorist attack spurred the United States and other countries around the world to develop new spying techniques, new cutting-edge equipment, and new, knowledgeable recruits to meet the challenge of 21st century enemies and threats.

In this book, you'll meet a few spies who have been exposed or caught, but most of today's spies still hide in the shadows, working against their enemies. So, here you'll get a glimpse of the new world of cyber spies and secret agents, and will learn along the way that anyone could be a spy next door. Even better, you might just learn that you have the skills of a modern-day spy—how will you use your new-found talents?

Terrorists attacked the World Trade Center in New York City on September 11, 2001.

CHAPTER 1

GAME CHANGER: HOW SEPTEMBER 11 CHANGED THE SPY WORLD

The last thing the Catholic priest, Father Jean-Marie Benjamin, expected was to become a spy. He didn't know that in early September 2001, in Todi, Italy, he would do just that. The day began as a joyful one—he married a young couple and was enjoying their wedding reception. During the celebration, one of the guests sidled up to him. The man whispered to Father Benjamin that something terrible was about to happen. An Islamist terrorist group was planning a deadly attack on the United States. They were going to hijack passenger planes and use them as suicide weapons.

Why would anyone give an Italian priest this information? Father Benjamin happened to be an expert on Islamic culture. Before he became a priest he had worked for the United Nations. For years he had worked with various Islamic charities in Iraq. The question was what would he do with that information? Would he shrug it off as too incredible to be true? Or would he take it seriously?

Father Benjamin suspected the terrorist threat was real. In the days after the wedding, he went to several Italian politicians and a judge with this explosive news, begging them to take action. They were as alarmed as he was. But the wedding guest had not known when or exactly where the attacks would take place.

It turned out that Father Benjamin wasn't the only person who knew something was coming. Spies from around the world had been warned too. The moment that the anonymous wedding guest shared that information with Father Benjamin, the priest unwittingly became part of a mysterious new international network. The network included spies from around the world who had a dangerous secret: they'd heard that there would be an attack on the United States.

SPIES AROUND THE WORLD GET EARLY WARNINGS

The first clue that something was happening came in 1999— two years before the attack. British spies sent a secret report to the United States. The report said that the Islamist extremist group al-Qaida was planning some kind of terrorist attack with airplanes. In the months leading up to 9/11, other spies around the world began hearing disturbing intelligence of a big attack that was being planned. In June, German agents warned the United States, Israel, and Great Britain of a plan that Middle Eastern

DID YOU KNOW?

Al-Qaida is an international terrorist group, founded by Osama bin Laden and other radical Islamists. Bin Laden formed the group in the 1980s when Afghanistan was at war with the Soviet Union. After the war, al-Qaida became a terrorist force fighting against all governments that it believed to be anti-Islamist, including the United States.

Osama Bin Laden was the mastermind behind the 9/11 attacks.

terrorist groups would use hijacked planes as bombs. In July, an Egyptian secret agent undercover in Afghanistan, reported that 20 al-Qaida members were in the United States training to fly small airplanes. Egyptian intelligence passed the information to the United States, but no one acted on the information.

Warnings continued to trickle in from around the world. A Moroccan undercover agent who had joined al-Qaida sent a message to the United States saying bin Laden was planning a huge attack in the fall. Intelligence agents in the country of Jordan intercepted a secret message that said a big attack on the United States was coming. According to the message, terrorists would use airplanes to attack somewhere inside the United States. The agent even knew the secret code name for the attack: Big Wedding.

Russian agents began hearing intel of an attack, too. According to the Russian spies, terrorists were training to fly suicide missions into U.S. targets. Those warnings also went straight to U.S. intelligence agencies. In August 2001, only a few weeks before Father Benjamin got his news, British agents sent two more warnings of al-Qaida hijackings in the United States to then-Prime Minister Tony Blair.

Some U.S. agents took the threats seriously. On August 6, 2001, Central Intelligence Agency (CIA) operatives gave President George W. Bush a paper titled, "Bin Laden Determined to Strike in U.S." But no actions were taken.

AN INTELLIGENCE DISASTER

On September 11, 2001, all the international warnings came terribly true. Al-Qaida operatives who had been living undercover in the United States hijacked four commercial U.S. airplanes. Their leader, Osama bin Laden, had given them their suicide mission: to attack and destroy the World Trade Center in New York City and the Pentagon and the White House in Washington, D.C. Three of their hijacked planes hit their targets and one crashed in a Pennsylvania field.

How could a well-known international terrorist group launch the biggest surprise attack on the United States since World War II? Especially since the United States had so many warnings from spies around the world. The 9/11 attacks turned out to be an enormous U.S. intelligence failure.

Why didn't anyone listen to the warnings from international spies? U.S. intelligence agencies didn't really believe the threat. They didn't have operatives in the field to confirm all the warnings. Instead, they had to rely on international spies, and those spies didn't have specifics, such as what day the attack was to happen, or what city was the target. The information from around the world was never put together in one place in the United States, so no specific agency had the full picture of what bin Laden was planning. Some agents had some pieces of information, while others got different intel. This failure to communicate allowed the

The United States Pentagon, which houses the U.S. Department of
Defense, was one of the targets in the 9/11 attacks.

attackers to take the United States by surprise.

Actual U.S. spies were also in short supply. In the 1990s, the
CIA and other intelligence organizations weren't sure who to spy
on any more. The Cold War with the former Soviet Union—now
broken up into Russia and several other countries—was over. The
United States no longer had any traditional enemies. The CIA and
other agencies recruited fewer agents and started relying more on
computers and cyber spying. Slowly, many of the vital human
connections with international agents disappeared. New agents
were too busy monitoring Internet threats to cultivate important
human allies and contacts around the world. After 9/11, U.S.
intelligence organizations realized that had been a big mistake.

A NEW WORLD OF SECRETS AND SPIES

Spying is one of the oldest jobs in the world. Powerful people always want to know what other powerful people are up to. Until the late 20th century, the way people spied on each other stayed pretty much the same. Secret codes, hidden messages, undercover surveillance, and old-fashioned tricks, such as disguises, were the tools of all the world's spies. In 2001, though, it was clear that other techniques of spying were needed as well.

The 9/11 attacks broke open the secret world of U.S. spies in the CIA and other government agencies. The CIA, FBI, and other U.S. intelligence agencies were riddled with problems.

A SPY'S LIFE MYTHS: Q & A

Q: Will I have to work out every day?

. A: Not unless you want to. Secret agents don't have superhuman strength. But they are intelligent and able to make thoughtful decisions. Think Black Widow, not the Hulk.

Officials were slow to adopt new technologies and ideas. This Cold War mind-set wasn't going to work anymore.

Although many different international spies heard intel about 9/11, the information was fragmented and incomplete. Reports went to different agencies, just as in the United States. After the attacks on 9/11, it was easy to look back and see how many warnings had come in. But at the time no one knew to connect the dots, or even how many dots there were.

Today, world threats no longer come from single, big countries or gory world wars. Spies from around the world battle shadowy, unseen enemies who work in small and relatively independent groups spread out over many different countries. These terrorists use their spy craft globally, taking advantage of the Internet to infiltrate their enemies. Today, one person with a laptop can bring down a country.

U.S. intelligence agencies learned their lessons from 9/11, and international spy groups also paid attention. Within the U.S. organizations, agents share more intel. A U.S. government organization, the National Counterterrorism Center (NCC), was created in 2003 just so the different agencies could communicate. The NCC is made up of high-level agents from many different agencies. Their goal is to share intelligence within the United States, and with agencies around the world whether they're U.S. agents working for the CIA, British agents with the Secret

Intelligence Service (MI6), or French agents with the General Directorate for External Security (DGSE), to try to ensure no one is caught by surprise by a big attack again.

WHEN IS A SPY NOT "A SPY"?

Not all clandestine operatives are called "spies," even though they're all working deep within the spy world. Say you're working for the CIA in a foreign country. You don't look or sound anything like the local people, but you need to get information without raising suspicion. How do you do it? Find someone to do the spying for you. You, the CIA operative who recruits new local spies, are not a spy. You're an officer (or handler, or core collector). Who are the spies? The locals you recruit to work for you. They are called agents (or assets, or spies) and they're the ones who will do all the spying. The handler trains the new agent, and then sends him or her off to gather intel. People often use "spy" and "officer" interchangeably, or use the term "spy" to indicate any undercover operative, though technically there are different terms for different jobs within the clandestine community.

Anna Chapman was part of an extensive undercover group of Russian spies living in the United States.

CHAPTER 2

FAKE CITIZENS, FAKE LIVES: HIDING IN PLAIN SIGHT

The grainy FBI surveillance video began by showing an empty staircase. Then a man appeared, carrying shopping bags. He started to climb. A second man appeared at the top of the staircase, going down. He also carried a handful of bags. So far, nothing unusual: just two strangers minding their own business after a day of shopping. Then the video got interesting. As the two figures passed on the staircase, they quickly switched bags without stopping. A few seconds later, they disappeared.

Those men weren't innocent shoppers. They were Russian agents, part of a sleeper cell of spies in the United States. Their mission? To go undercover, living as Americans, to send as much secret information back to Russia as they could. That bag-switching move, called a brush-pass, is something spies use all the time to exchange information.

Eleven Russian spies had come to the United States undercover to gather information. They had signed on for the mission knowing that it would go on for years. It's not clear exactly when they arrived in the United States but some had already begun their mission as far back as 2001, possibly even earlier than that.

They were instructed to become part of American society, so no one would ever suspect they were highly trained, expert agents. Their long-term mission was to infiltrate political circles and make contacts with people in the U.S. government. They were to gather information on U.S. nuclear weapons, rumors and information on Congress, the White House, and U.S. foreign policy.

What they didn't know was that the FBI had been on to them from the beginning. For 10 years U.S. spies watched the Russians' every move. They set up dozens of video surveillance cameras and watched their calls and emails. On June 27, 2010, the FBI ended the Russian spies' mission by arresting 10 of the 11 spies (one spy, known as Christopher Metsos, escaped and is still at large). The spies' names and photos were splashed all over the Internet and in newspapers around the world. It was the biggest Russian spy roundup in the United States in more than 20 years.

NORMAL PEOPLE, SECRET LIVES

The first thing people noticed about these highly secretive, deeply dangerous spies was how normal they looked. Male and female agents worked as undercover husband and wife teams, and some of them had children together. They went to school, bought houses, and had everyday jobs. To everyone they met, they seemed like ordinary, even boring, American families.

Hidden in their normal-looking lives, they used a mix of old spy tricks and modern technology to gather information and pass it on. The "brush pass" was only one of the dozens of ways they passed information to their Russian handlers. They used invisible ink and secret codes to pass messages, and kept hidden codebooks. Each agent used complex passwords to identify each other. One coded phrase was, "Excuse me, but haven't we met in California last summer?" The password reply was "No, I think it was in the Hamptons." They gave their contacts code names like Cat and Parrot.

The arrest by the FBI of 10 spies living undercover in the United States made headline news.

DID YOU KNOW?

The FBI called their surveillance
operation on the Russian spies
"Operation Ghost Stories" because six
of the Russian spies had stolen the
identities of dead people.

One of their favorite ways to pass information was by sitting in outdoor coffee shops or bookstores with their laptops. Who would suspect someone sipping coffee and surfing the Internet? Their Russian contacts would drive by slowly. The spies then beamed information from their computers to the contacts' electronic devices. Sometimes they hid encrypted information in photos and then posted the photos online.

WHAT MAKES A GOOD SPY?

When the FBI arrested the Russian spies in 2010, one stood out to the public. Anna Chapman was a young, attractive redhead who perfectly fit the "sexy spy" profile. She soon became a celebrity worldwide. Chapman used her fame to become a model, and eventually to host her own Russian TV show. But while the world was taken with her good looks, they glossed over the real story: Chapman, like her fellow Russian agents, was an intelligent, highly trained spy. She and the other spies were chosen for the U.S. mission because of their skills with the English language and the ease with which they could adapt to other cultures.

Chapman and her fellow Russian spies were the cream of the spy crop in Russia. What do spies like Anna Chapman, and other international agents, have that no one else has?

Spies are supersmart. Chapman has an IQ of 162—an IQ considered to be "genius"—and earned a master's degree in economics while in Russia. But "smart" doesn't always mean "college degree." Take "Shami" (not his real name). He is a British secret agent who never went to college. It was his street smarts that made him perfect for his spy job. He conducts secret surveillance on suspected terrorist cells for MI5, the British Security Service.

But the most important thing that makes a good spy is honesty and integrity. That may sound strange, since it's in the spy job description to lie and cheat—and they must do that all the time. But a spy also has to be trustworthy, someone a contact, or another spy, will respect enough to pass information to and even risk their lives for. Open, pleasant people who make friends easily

A SPY'S LIFE MYTHS: Q & A

Q: I'll never see my friends and family again, right?

A: Your job is a secret, but you'll still have a life. You might travel around the world, or you might work in a cubicle every day. Either way, you can have a family and friends.

DID YOU KNOW?

Most secret agents don't have the
power to arrest anyone. When it's
time to arrest the bad guy, an agent
has to call the police just like
everyone else.

make great spies. Anna Chapman and the other Russian agents were great at this. Their mission was to become "American," and they did it so well that when they were arrested, their American friends and neighbors were stunned. All the spies lived in normal suburban neighborhoods. Two of the Russians, Michael Zottoli (Mikhail Kutsik) and Patricia Mills (Natalia Pereverzeva) used to take walks through their Seattle neighborhood with their son. Another spy, Mikhail Semenko, posted online that he loved the New Jersey Devils hockey team. Cynthia Murphy (Lydia Guryev) loved gardening and planted hydrangeas in her yard while her two daughters rode their bikes. If this all sounds normal and boring, it's supposed to. The less threatening a spy is, the better chance he or she will have to gain someone's trust.

As well as infiltrating "normal" neighborhoods in the United States, the sleeper Russian agents relied on high-tech spying. Their Russian-made laptops were secretly loaded with a private wireless network that only communicated with the other spies' computers. They exchanged information and

Cynthia Murphy (Lydia Guryev) was a Russian undercover spy in the United States for many years.

kept records of their spy activities on the laptops. The FBI needed those laptops, and they found a way to get them. An undercover agent posed as a Russian-speaking fellow spy and offered to fix one laptop that wasn't working properly. The Russian agent fell for his story and handed over the laptop. The whole spy ring was arrested a few weeks later.

Although the Russian spy ring never got their hands on any real, secret intelligence, they came dangerously close. Eventually, all the Russians were exchanged for several U.S. spies that the Russian government had caught.

A SPY'S LIFE MYTHS: Q & A

Q: Do I have to speak several foreign languages?

A: If you can, all the better. If not, it's not a problem. If you get a mission in which you do need to know another language, you'll learn it.

Spying in the digital age adds a new dimension to gathering information.

CHAPTER 3

WORLD THREAT: CYBER SPYING

Spies know each other. Or maybe they don't. They work together in groups. Or they work alone. They sit in dark rooms, bent over glowing computer screens. Or they hang out in brightly lit cafés. No one knows. Cyber spy groups are some of the biggest threats to world security. The scary part is that no one knows who they are, where they live, or how they work.

One international spy ring, purported to be the biggest in the world, has an innocent-sounding name: Emissary Panda. But what they do is anything but cute and cuddly. This shadowy group of cyber spies has been stealing information from military and political organizations around the world. They've taken emails, documents, data, and records that could destroy organizations. Their hacking mission is called Iron Tiger. No one knows who the members of Emissary Panda are, but they are based in China.

Emissary Panda, also known as Threat Group 3390, started by attacking companies in Asia. By 2013, they got bolder, hacking into the computer systems of high-tech companies in Europe and the United States. They also targeted embassies and organizations located in Russia, Iraq, Italy, Zambia, Afghanistan, and other countries in Africa, Europe, and the Middle East. They knew exactly what they were doing, targeting specific companies that specialized in military, intelligence, nuclear engineering, and communications. They chose their victims carefully and spent years getting into systems that held the most secret information.

Alarmingly, Emissary Panda changed their strategy around 2014. Before that, they would take everything they could find. Suddenly the spies slowed down, taking as long as two weeks to explore a hacked system and make long lists of the data they found. Then they'd carefully choose very specific files to steal.

THE FIRST CYBER SPY

In 1986, a German hacker named Markus Hess was recruited by the KGB, the Russian secret police. Hess' top-secret mission: to hack into world military and government systems and steal secrets. Hess managed to break into 30 computer systems in West Germany, Japan, and the United States and then sell the information to the KGB. He was caught and found guilty of

For instance, a system might have thousands of secret files, but Emissary Panda would only steal two or three. That means the group is probably not stealing to make money. No one knows what the hacking group is doing with the information, but it's possible that they're working for someone, or some group, who tells them what to take.

Emissary Panda isn't the only world cyber spy group hacking its way through global computer systems. A Russian-speaking spy group launched a huge cyber attack around 2007. U.S. counterspies dubbed it "Red October," after a 1990 U.S. film called *The Hunt for Red October.* These Red October spies had very specific goals in mind: stealing information from diplomatic agencies around the world. They mostly targeted countries in Eastern Europe and Asia, but evidence of their spying has turned up in Western European and U.S. systems, too. Their victims are government agencies, embassies, consulates, and scientific research groups that have government and military secrets.

WORLD SPY CYBER TRICKS

Emissary Panda and Red October spies might have been from different countries but they used the same cyber spy tricks to steal secrets. The easiest was a trick called "spear phishing" to get passwords and other information used to break into computer systems. First they targeted specific people who had access to secrets and classified intelligence. The spies looked them up on social media to find out things such as the restaurants they went to, where they shopped, and who their friends were.

Then the real spying started. Emissary Panda sent fake emails to their targets. The emails looked like they were from friends, or from places that person had visited. Buried inside those emails was spyware that was automatically downloaded into the target's computer. The spyware let the spies break into that computer and get into the entire system. From there, they stole more classified information, passwords, and codes, and used those to break into other systems.

Both sets of international spies knew that most of the stolen intelligence would not be well protected. Even the best security programs can have bugs and holes that good hackers can find. Although the spies were experienced hackers, it didn't take much effort to get what they wanted.

The Iron Tiger hack wasn't a total surprise to the CIA and other U.S. spies. The Red October attack didn't come as a big surprise to European leaders, either. They'd been working to protect government computers from this kind of global cyber attack for years. After 9/11, the CIA and other world agencies became even more convinced that the next attacks would come from the Internet. Terrorist groups, they thought, would use the Internet to break into organizations and do physical damage to industry, communications, or transportation systems around the world. Cyber agents were trained to watch for these threats.

So far, there has been only one cyber terrorism attack like that anywhere in the world. In 2010, an Iranian nuclear power plant was attacked by Stuxnet, a virus that broke down machinery and computer systems. However, cyber spies are generally more interested in information, secrets, and classified documents. Cyber espionage remains the big threat of the 21st century.

EDWARD SNOWDEN: THE ULTIMATE CYBER SPY

On May 20, 2013, a quiet man boarded a plane traveling from the United States to Hong Kong. A few days later, in Hong Kong, he met with journalists from the United Kingdom. He told them his name was Edward Snowden, and he used to work with the U.S. National Security Agency (NSA). As part of his computer job at the NSA, he saw top-secret files. He stole them—millions of them—and then fled the country.

Why did he steal the files? The files revealed that the NSA was spying on ordinary Americans. The more Snowden saw how much the United States was spying on its own citizens, the angrier he got. He finally decided to do something about it by revealing those secrets to the world. The stolen files revealed how large U.S. companies such as Microsoft and Verizon gave the

Edward Snowden stole millions of cyber documents from the NSA.

NSA vast amounts of data and information on their customers.

Snowden revealed even more disturbing information about NSA spying. The NSA spied on computers that weren't connected to the Internet. The NSA paid software companies millions of dollars to create security programs with a "back door," allowing the NSA to spy on any company that used them. The NSA even tapped the phone calls of world leaders.

Journalists published Snowden's story and the world exploded at the news. The U.S. government charged Snowden with "theft of government property" and other charges under the Espionage Act. Not long after the leaks went public, Snowden disappeared from Hong Kong.

Eventually, Snowden arrived in Russia, where he lives today. Snowden continues to release these documents, and he says he has millions more.

DID YOU KNOW?

A movie called *Snowden* was released
in 2016 about Edward Snowden's cyber
spying. An NSA retired deputy director
said the movie exaggerated many things
and mischaracterized the NSA.

SPIES ON THE HUNT

One of the best ways cyber agents collect information is through cyber cafés. A cyber café is a shop, anywhere in the world, filled with computers that anyone can use for a small fee. Cyber cafés are often tucked away on side streets of cities such as London, Paris, Bangkok, Beijing, Cairo, and others. Many of them are near foreign embassies, religious buildings, international businesses, and other places a terrorist might frequent.

Most people who use cyber cafés think they are safe and anonymous. The reality is that some international cyber cafés were built by U.S. and British cyber agents. They watched what

OLD-SCHOOL SPYING MEETS COMPUTER TECH

Most world cyber agents spy on terrorist groups using both old-school spying skills and 21st century computer technology. The old fashioned, but very useful "dead drop" trick is perfect for cyber spies. One spy goes to a cyber café, library, or other public spot with Internet and downloads information into a public computer. The second spy comes along later and uploads that information. Sometimes the secret info is embedded in innocent looking emails, or in hidden codes within documents or photos.

websites people visited, monitored their browser history, recorded passwords and logins, and even planted spyware. It was a great way to look for terrorist activity.

U.S. agents closed most of their fake cyber cafés but they still use some to communicate with other foreign agents. In 2013, American spy Ryan Fogle was caught by Russian agents. They accused him of trying to recruit a Russian counter-agent to pass secrets to the U.S. government. The proof? A letter from him to his Russian counter-agent that explained how to make contact at a cyber café.

We operate around the world to make this country safer and more prosperous. As you can imagine it's no easy task. So whether we need a thoroughly efficient administrator or an overseas operator in the field, we hire people we can depend on because everyone in the UK depends on them. For more details about joining Britain's secret intelligence service, go to **www.siscareers.gov.uk**

Agencies around the world will sometimes advertise for good recruits for clandestine work.

CHAPTER 4

CLANDESTINE RECRUITING: LOOKING FOR A FEW GOOD SPIES

Spy Camp. It sounded like the coolest summer camp ever to a specially select group of Washington, D.C., high school students. In the summer of 2005, the students spent a week at Spy Camp. Instead of swimming and canoeing, the group went behind the scenes at CIA headquarters in Langley, Virginia. Rather than doing arts and crafts, they toured the Spy Museum and joined in scavenger hunts where teams had to practice code breaking and other spy skills.

The teens didn't know it, but the camp wasn't just for fun. It was created by Trinity University in Washington D.C., and a U.S. spy agency called the Office of National Intelligence (ONI). Its purpose is to find and recruit new spies. Spy Camp was part of a bigger program: the Intelligence Community Centers for Academic Excellence.

Today there are more than 20 spy camps (now called Summer Intelligence Seminars) and other secret agent camps

Students in Spy Camp work together to solve different problems.

on college campuses around the United States every summer. Some have high school programs, where kids learn spy tricks, such as using GPS to locate hidden (not real) weapons of mass destruction around a city.

The ONI didn't expect anyone to drop out of school and become a spy. But finding future secret agents is serious business for spy agencies all over the world, not just in the United States.

THE SECRET TO FINDING SECRET AGENTS

Most of the time, finding good spies is like finding good people to work in any job. The secret is that looking for them isn't a secret at all.

The big spy agencies like the CIA and Britain's MI6 go all out to find recruits. In 2011, Britain's top code-cracking and spy organization, Government Communications Headquarters (GCHQ), took recruitment online. They created a website called "Can You Crack It" with a mysterious cryptographic puzzle. The site challenged anyone to solve it. The lucky few who cracked the code were rewarded with a secret congratulatory message and the link to another website where the person could apply for a job as a code-cracking spy with GCHQ.

Spy groups don't just use camps and codes to find new agents. World espionage organizations have websites and YouTube commercials showing how awesome being a spy can be. In 2015, the British spy agency MI6 launched a huge recruitment campaign linked to the release of the James Bond movie *Spectre*. The campaign asked for recruits who wanted to "explore the human side of global intelligence."

In 2016, Britain's Ministry of Defence put an ad in the British Army's official magazine, *Soldier*. The advertisement showed a woman standing at a bus stop reading a newspaper. Next to it, a caption read: "This woman has vital information . . . Do you have the skills to find out what it is?"

A secret military group called the Defence Human Intelligence Unit (DHU) was behind the ad. They were looking for volunteers to fight ISIS and other terrorist groups. But the recruits wouldn't be shipped overseas. These secret agents would work on the streets of the United Kingdom. The DHU's agents would go undercover all over Britain, dressed in plainclothes, and no one would know who they were. Their only job would be to observe and record events as they happened on the street, in real time.

SPY SKILLS 101

Even if you are a master hacker or a code breaker, there are some basic requirements to being a spy in most countries. You have to be a citizen of the country you want to spy for. There's usually an age requirement, and some countries such as the United States would prefer agents with university degrees. Recruits usually have to pass a drug test, a credit check, and a criminal background check. They might have to take a lie-detector test. All of that is just the first step.

Recruits who meet those requirements move on to the next step. Spies don't have to speak different languages, but they do have to be skilled at learning them. Additionally, good spies have good social skills and can make friends easily.

The next part is trickier. No matter what country you're spying for, only recruits who can handle high stress and daily pressure will make it through. Can you go without sleep for long periods of time? How do you handle discomfort? What will you do when faced with instant danger? If you can think on your feet and stay cool-headed in a crisis, you might be spy material.

Finally, many spies must work undercover, so recruits have to be willing to lie to everyone they know, including friends, family, and coworkers (if they have a "cover" job). It may sound easy, but this part is sometimes the hardest to do. If you're good at hiding the truth, then you could be a spy.

GLOBAL SPY SCHOOLS THAT DON'T EXIST

The Farm. Fort Monckton. The University. These boring-sounding facilities hide a huge secret: each one of them is a secret spy school somewhere in the world. New recruits are sent to these schools to learn the top-secret tricks to being a world-class agent.

The Farm, near Williamsburg, Virginia, is the CIA training camp where U.S. recruits learn the business of spying. The camp is surrounded by a chain-link fence and no one is allowed in or out without permission. Fort Monckton, near Gosport, Hampshire, is the British ground zero for spy training. It's a real stone fort, and recruits must enter through an ancient drawbridge. The University, in Germany, is a sprawling facility in a secret location that few outside the German secret service know about.

Secret spy schools might be spread across the globe, but their spies-in-training have a lot in common. They all have to take classes with cool-sounding names like "Picks and Locks,"

"Code Breaking," and "Breaking and Entering." Recruits learn how to bug phones, read maps, exchange packages, open sealed envelopes, and interrogate suspects. At The University, German recruits focus on legal questions such as how to deal with a kidnapping in a foreign country. They study history, religion, politics, and geography. They learn how to recognize a liar. And that's just the classroom work.

On the outdoor training grounds at Fort Monckton and The Farm, British and U.S. recruits learn how to assemble and shoot different weapons, learn about different kinds of foreign weapons, and practice handling explosives. They train to shoot in every kind of weather condition and climate, from desert to blizzard. At the Farm, they spend hours training in hand-to-hand combat and martial arts skills such as krav maga and jiu jitsu.

Modern spies usually don't find themselves in dramatic car chases like in the movies, but in case they do, they learn how to drive and survive. Recruits at The Farm and The University learn how to use their car as a weapon or as protection from terrorists. At The Farm, U.S. recruits learn how to spin their own car and how to drive from the passenger seat if their driver is shot dead. Escape training includes high-speed driving around corners without losing control of the car.

Once a recruit graduates from any of these spy schools, it's time to go out into the field. Each U.S. recruit is assigned a city where former undercover FBI agents try to discover them and blow their cover. Recruits who pass this final test are official secret agents.

SPIES FINDING SPIES

An officer's hardest job is finding recruits from other countries who are willing to pass secrets. Every officer needs to establish trusted contacts around the world. Recruiting spies for their personal spy network is job number one.

First, an officer identifies the kinds of information she wants. The officer can target an individual who might have that information, or she can find a "principal agent" to help.

A SPY'S LIFE MYTHS: Q & A

Q: Will I get a fast car?

A: Car chases aren't part of a spy's job description. But you will learn how to drive any type of car to escape danger—no "fast" cars needed.

VALERIE PLAME

She was a U.S. government employee stationed in Athens, Greece, like dozens of other ordinary officials. That was her cover, anyway. But Valerie Plame wasn't in Greece to push papers and go to meetings. She was an undercover officer, sent abroad to recruit new spies for the United States.

Valerie, who was recruited by the CIA right out of college, spent years as a secret agent all over the world. She was the perfect spy: smart, capable, and not afraid of either danger or the loneliness that is part of a spy's life. By the mid-1990s she became one of the CIA's top NOCs (non-official cover agents). NOCs are the most secret of secret agents. They are the same as Russia's "illegals" or other countries' deep-cover spies. They don't have cover government jobs to keep their identities safe. Even more dangerous, the United States doesn't acknowledge them at all and gives them no protection. Valerie told everyone she was a businesswoman with an international company, but she still recruited spies for the United States.

It all went bad in the summer of 2003. The Bush administration claimed Iraq's leader, Saddam Hussein, had weapons of mass destruction. U.S. spies, however, couldn't find evidence of any weapons. In July, Valerie's husband, former ambassador Joe Wilson, wrote a newspaper article that accused the administration of making up evidence to justify war. Someone in the Bush administration leaked to the press that Valerie was an undercover agent; according to Joe Wilson and many others, her name was leaked in retaliation for Wilson's article. Valerie's cover was blown and her days as a secret agent were over. She wrote a book, *Fair Game* (that later became a movie by the same name), about her experiences, and now lives a quiet life with Joe in Santa Fe, New Mexico, far from the spy world she once lived in.

The principal agent is someone who fits into the group or culture and speaks the same language. That person scouts around to find others in the group who might be interested in turning into a spy.

For German spies, getting sources is one of their top jobs. One German spy had a tough assignment: recruiting an asset and getting him to trust her. She only had an hour and a half to do it. In that time she managed to find out about his job, his hobbies, and even his daughter's college test scores. She gained his trust, and with it, a new recruit.

Another way spies get other spies on their side is through "walk-ins." These people ask to join up and steal secrets from their countries. They do this for a lot of reasons. Most of them want money for their secrets. Some are angry at their companies, or their government, and want to punish them.

Once these new spies are recruited, they learn how to secretly pass along the information they've been asked to steal. Often the spy will have a secret location or a safe house where they can meet their officer to get assignments and exchange information.

Those who work at the U.S. National Reconnaissance Office design and build spy satellites.

CHAPTER 5

SPYING IN THE 21ST CENTURY AND BEYOND

Today's enemies are not just big armies or scary governments with nuclear weapons. Terrorist groups are small, mobile, and anonymous. They can stay invisible until they attack, and then do tremendous damage. These groups can be anywhere, at any time. They don't play by any of the rules that most governments are used to.

Spies in the 21st century must be trained to meet these new threats. They don't want to go to war—their job is to do everything they can to avoid it. To do that, every country needs information to run their governments and to watch for enemies. Global spies must know how to get any kind of information, anywhere, at any time. Where is all this new information coming from? Modern spies put a new spin on all the old tricks spies have always used, including human contacts, high-tech spying, and good old-fashioned research to meet new 21st century threats.

HUMINT: PERSON-TO-PERSON SPYING

HUMINT, or human intelligence, forms the basis of spying. Human officers gather information on the ground by creating relationships and trust with sources and other spies. Today, many officials believe that HUMINT is more important than ever, both for the United States and the world spy community.

How does HUMINT work? An agent gets a tip from an informant or a friend—a human source. Sometimes that means interrogating a witness. Other HUMINT can come from espionage or other secret sources. Most countries have their own intelligence divisions that focus on HUMINT. In the United States, HUMINT gathering is the job of the CIA. In Britain, MI6 is responsible for HUMINT.

The United States has been behind in HUMINT compared to other countries, mainly because U.S. agents concentrated on using technology to spy during the Cold War. France, China, and Russia have strong, well-established HUMINT capabilities around the world.

SIGINT: SPY FROM THE SKY

Ever heard of spy satellites? They collect SIGINT, or Signals Intelligence, which is information sent electronically. Ships, planes, computers, and satellites gather SIGINT every day. The United States is ahead of everyone else in the world when it comes to SIGINT. There's even a special U.S. intelligence agency, the National Reconnaissance Office, that employs people to build and maintain U.S. spy satellites.

U.S. SIGINT gathering is so advanced because it started more than 60 years ago, during the space race in the late 1950s in the midst of the Cold War. In 1959, a series of rockets blasted off from Onizuka Air Force Station in California. The National Aeronautics and Space Administration (NASA) told the press it was a mission called Discoverer. The Discoverer rockets were designed to test engineering systems, launching systems, and other systems needed for space flight.

A SPY'S LIFE MYTHS: Q & A

Q: I can't wait to get all the spy gadgets. I do get gadgets, don't I?

A: Agents do use cool technology as well as old-school spyware, such as invisible ink and hollow pens. When you get an assignment, you get the gadgets that are needed to go with it. What kind of gadgets will you have? That's classified.

Rockets take satellites to space.

The top-secret information NASA didn't share with the world was that Discoverer was a code name for a project even more secret. The project was so undercover that it had a second code name: Corona. The Corona program was a secret spy mission to send cameras into space using Corona satellites. The Corona was the United States' first spy satellite. It's biggest mission: to spy on the Soviet Union.

Deep inside those Discoverer rockets were their true payload: Corona spy satellites equipped with two 5-foot-long (1.5-m-long) cameras. The cameras were so high-tech that they could take clear black-and-white, 3-foot (1-m) close-ups of anything on Earth.

Since then, the United States and other countries have launched dozens of spy satellites into orbit. But it's not just about photos any more. In today's high-tech world, SIGINT includes the kind of information a spy can gather electronically. A basic spy trick all intelligence agencies use involves tapping phone lines and secretly listening in on conversations. SIGINT spy satellites do that on a global scale.

These satellites detect and monitor every kind of broadcast communication: radio, television, telephone, electronic systems,

SOLVING THE MYSTERY OF MALAYSIA FLIGHT 17 WITH MASINT

On July 17, 2014, a Malaysia Airlines commercial flight was downed over Ukraine, killing 283 passengers and 15 crew members. Immediately, world spy agencies suspected that the plane was shot down by a missile. But how could they prove it? With MASINT (spying on weapons), spy satellites can detect a missile launch anywhere in the world, tracking it by its heat signature. U.S. spies analyzed this data from satellites to determine that the missile was a Soviet-era Buk missile, launched either from Russia or Ukraine. Both governments admit they use Buk missiles, but both also denied they shot down the plane. No definitive answer has been found at this time.

and even other satellites. They can also follow electronic transmissions from weapons tests or enemy radar systems. They can pinpoint locations where the broadcasts or messages come from, and their computer systems can decrypt coded messages. The only downside to these powerful spy satellites is that they can't pick up messages sent on landlines such as fiber-optic underground or undersea cables.

France, Italy, and Germany all have a few spy satellites in orbit and some spy networks on land and sea in Europe and around the world. But these countries' spies are best in HUMINT. That puts agents in a good position to trade secrets, exchanging intel gathered through SIGINT in return for information gathered from HUMINT sources.

MASINT: SPYING ON WEAPONS

How can you spy on a weapon? One word: technology. High-tech weapons send information and data through their computer systems. Specially trained spies can hack into the weapons' computer systems, and use Measurement and Signature Intelligence (MASINT) to steal or monitor useful information, such as where the weapons are, how they work, and what they target. Then the agents analyze the data to get the most information. For instance, MASINT can be used to find chemical weapons, or to identify chemical parts of unknown weapons.

MASINT comes in many different ways. For instance, acoustic intel is information based on sound. Different weapons or systems make different sounds, clueing a spy in on which weapon is making that noise without seeing the weapon itself. Seismic intel can be ground-shaking—literally. Agents monitor how much the ground shakes when a weapons target rolls past to determine its size and strength.

OSINT: INTEL IN PLAIN SIGHT

Facebook, Twitter, Tumblr, Snapchat, television, radio, magazine articles, reports, speeches, newspapers, and public records are everywhere. The best spies know how to get information from these public, or open, sources, called Open Source Intel (OSINT). Most agents use a combination of OSINT and other intelligence gathering to get as much information as possible. Government spy organizations in the United States, Britain, Australia, Israel, China, and Russia all have OSINT divisions. But it's not just spies who use OSINT. Because terrorists can strike anywhere, in any city in the world, law-enforcement agencies such as Interpol (Europe), Scotland Yard (Britain), the Royal Canadian Mounted Police, and police departments in New York and Chicago (United States) have created OSINT squads.

Sometimes the Internet makes it easy for anyone, not just agents, to spy on the world. Google Earth was a big game-changer in the global world of OSINT spying. Now anyone can look in on any country on Earth, and see whether it is gathering an army or building weapons. The best OSINT targets are organizations in countries that have good Internet and telecommunications. In an era when terrorist groups have their own magazines and YouTube channels, it's not hard to find and monitor world threats with OSINT.

The problem is that there is so much information it can be hard for an intelligence analyst to figure out what's most important. They spend hours, or days, surfing the Internet, looking for bits of intel that might help them with a mission. Most OSINT spies are good at foreign languages, so they can read websites and intel from many countries.

MODERN SPY GADGETS

Today's spies use the latest gear in their classified missions. A lot of their technology involves 21st century versions of the best spy tricks agents have used for years.

Back in the old-school spy days, "remote monitoring," or listening in on someone's conversations, meant planting electronic "bugs" in homes or on telephones. Back then that meant a spy had to break into a home or business, plant a bug in a hidden location, and hope no one found it. Today's global spies don't have to resort to breaking and entering (although they learn how to do so in spy school.) Dozens of everyday objects come already equipped with bugs. Does an agent need to put a secret surveillance camera in someone's home? Just pose as an electrician and install electrical outlets with their own hidden cameras. Even better is a fake smoke alarm that is really a video camera with a motion detector and night vision. Clocks, pens, buttons, neckties, and even air fresheners come with their own cameras and monitoring devices.

Sometimes spies need to break into someone's computer. The days when a cyber spy spent days, or weeks, trying to figure out passwords is long gone. Today's spies plant a keylogger on the computer. This handy spy gadget records every keystroke that anyone types, and keeps track of passwords and email. Sometimes an agent can load a keylogger program onto a computer. Keylogger software can be secretly installed from a website the spy has infected with the program. Other keyloggers are small devices that plug into the computer and send the information remotely.

Cyber spy groups like Emissary Panda and Red October used keyloggers to steal secrets. CIA and MI6 agents used them in fake cyber cafés to monitor users' emails and conversations.

Following a target has always been a basic spy job. Movies and TV shows are full of spies planting electronic tracking devices on cars. Modern spies now have high-tech GPS devices that can track everything from the route, speed, direction, and even altitude of a vehicle. Not only that, but all this information can be downloaded into the spy's computer and saved.

Ordinary writing pens have often been turned into some of the best spy gadgets. They can hold cameras, microphones, and recording devices. Today, secret spy pens can be used as document scanners, with the ability to quickly and clearly copy secret messages and other classified documents.

Most people carry loose change, and what better way to hide messages and secret information than in a coin? Hollow coins have been a spy's go-to gadget since the Cold War, and they're still as useful today as they were back then. Years ago spies used hollow coins to hide microfilm or suicide poison. Today's spies are more likely to hide a computer SD card. The biggest danger with these secret coins? Forgetting they're not real coins and spending them.

OLD-SCHOOL SPYING MAKING A COMEBACK

The more that spies rely on computers and other high-tech devices, the more they find out how unreliable they can be. The more that countries around the world rely on electronics and computers, the easier it becomes for anyone with a laptop to break into classified and secret files. Modern spies in the United States and Britain are packing away their computers and high-tech devices and returning to plain old HUMINT. What that means is spies are going back to using face-to-face meetings and hands-on surveillance. They're making connections in the real world with

DID YOU KNOW?

In 2018, a new super-spy reconnaissance
satellite will blast into space, code-named
NROL-71. It's so top secret and classified
that very few people know what kind of spy
tech this new satellite has.

real people to gather the intelligence they need.

Computer systems have become so easy to hack that most enemies and terrorist groups have taken vital information offline for good. Instead, they're communicating with old-fashioned codes, cyphers, secret messages, short-wave radio transmissions, and real-world dead drops. Not only are these spy tricks effective, they're also free. Terrorist networks that don't have a lot of money for high-tech computers or other gear use the old-school spy techniques. The best 21st century spies will be experts at mixing old-world tricks with modern tech to catch the bad guys.

Spy tools can be hidden in everyday objects.

Timeline

1959
The first spy satellites, code-named Corona, are launched

September 11, 2001
Terrorists hijack airplanes and fly them into both towers of the
World Trade Center in New York, the Pentagon in Washington,
D.C., and crashing in a field in Pennsylvania, killing almost 3,000
people

October 26, 2001
President George W. Bush signs the USA PATRIOT Act, which
gives U.S. spy agencies greater power to gather intelligence

2003
Valerie Plame is outed as a CIA agent

2010
Eleven Russian spies are arrested by the FBI and deported

2013
American spy Ryan Fogle is arrested in Russia. Emissary Panda
hackers break into classified government computer systems
throughout the United States. Edward Snowden leaks secret
classified information to the world

October 2015
The CIA creates a new cyber crime division, the Directorate of
Digital Innovation

Glossary

conspirators—people who plan to commit something, usually harmful or illegal, together

clandestine—done in secret

classified—confidential or secret

dead drop—a secret location where an agent leaves something for another agent to pick up

digital—in an electronic format

disguise—to hide by changing one's appearance or demeanor

eavesdrop—to secretly listen in on a conversation

encrypt—to encode a message

fiber optic—using various materials that use light signals to carry a large amount of information

hacker—a person who breaks into a computer network

handler—an intelligence officer who recruits a spy, and then trains and works with him or her

high-tech—advanced technology; short for high technology

infiltrate—to move into an area or group slowly and secretly

intel—short for intelligence

intelligence—information about an enemy

mischaracterize—to falsely describe something

operative—a secret agent or spy

purported—assumed to be true, but not necessarily so

SD card—a secure digital card that stores information

sidle—to move close to another person

surveillance—keeping watch on a person or location

telecommunications—communication via technology, as in through phones or the Internet

transmitter—a device for sending broadcasts

CRITICAL THINKING USING THE COMMON CORE

1. The 9/11 attacks revealed serious problems within the U.S. spy community. One of the biggest issues was that the different intelligence agencies "hoarded" their information and didn't share it. Why is sharing information a good idea? What might have happened differently had the different agencies talked about the clues they had that an attack would happen? Support your answer with at least two other sources. (Integration of Knowledge and Ideas)

2. Secret agents lead double lives. They have to lie and cheat every day, often to people they care about. However, being an agent requires a strict ethical code. What are the ethics that spies must have? Find examples in the text and from two other sources. (Craft and Structure)

3. Edward Snowden revealed that the NSA was illegally spying on ordinary Americans. The U.S. government insisted that it was necessary to do this, in order to catch terrorists. How far do you think the government should be allowed to go into the private lives of American citizens? Is the right to privacy less important than national security? Support your answer with at least two other sources. (Integration of Knowledge and Ideas)

ADDITIONAL RESOURCES

FURTHER READING

Briggs, Andy. *How to be an International Spy: Your Training Manual, Should You Choose to Accept It.* Lonely Planet Kids. New York: Lonely Planet, 2015.

Fardon, John. *100 Facts: Spies.* Essex, U.K.: Miles Kelly Publishing, 2015.

Johnson, Bud. *Break the Code: Cryptography for Beginners.* New York: Dover, 2013.

Price, Sean. *Modern Spies.* North Mankato, Minn.: Capstone Press, 2015.

INTERNET SITES

Use FactHound to find Internet sites related to this book. All of the sites on FactHound have been researched by our staff.

Here's all you do:
Visit *www.facthound.com*
Type in this code: 9780756554989

SOURCE NOTES

p. 10, lines 23–24, http://www.cnn.com/2004/ALLPOLITICS/04/10/august6.memo/

p. 19, lines 8–10, http://www.telegraph.co.uk/news/worldnews/europe/russia/7861456/Russian-spy-ring-guide-from-21st-Century-to-Cold-War-spy-novel.html

SELECT BIBLIOGRAPHY

Campbell, Stephen. "Intelligence in the Post-Cold War Period. Part II: The Impact of Technology." *The Intelligencer, Journal of U.S. Intelligence Studies* 20, no. 1 (2013): 57–65.
https://www.afio.com/publications/CAMPBELL%20Stephen%20Part%202%20of%20Guide%20to%20Intelligence%20in%20the%20Post-Cold%20War%20Period%20Part%20II%20Impact%20of%20Technology%20Final%20in%20Intelligencer.pdf

Central Intelligence Agency, https://www.cia.gov/index.html

Federal Bureau of Investigation, https://www.fbi.gov

National Reconnaissance Office, http://nro.gov

Schindler, John R. "The Truth about Spywar and How 21st Century Espionage Really Works." *The Observer*, December 21, 2015.
http://observer.com/2015/12/the-truth-about-spywar-and-how-21st-century-espionage-really-works/

INDEX

ABOUT THE AUTHOR

Allison Lassieur loves digging up dangerous facts about secret agents in the safety of her office in west Tennessee. She has written more than 100 books about history, science, the unexplained, and famous people.